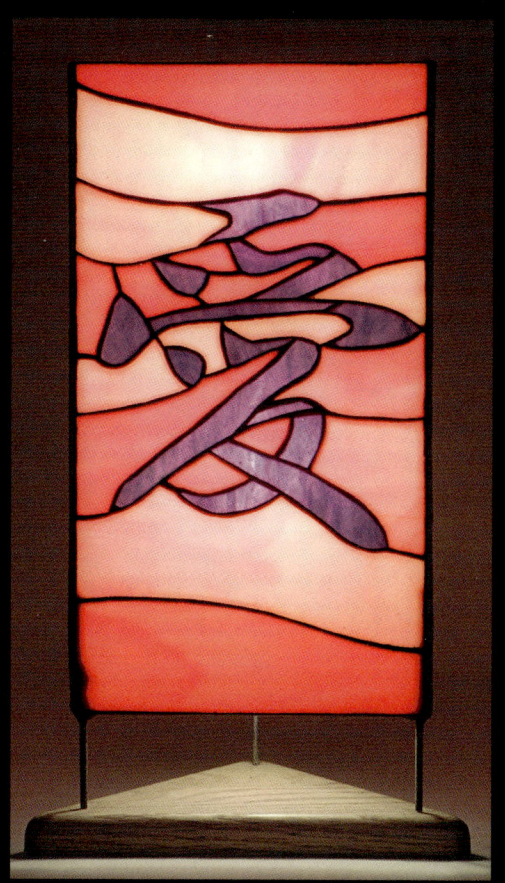
Ai (Love) - P.5

Morning Glory - P.20

Mice - P.19

Platypus - P.24

Cypress - P.10

Kingfisher - P.16

Aanraku Stained Glass
Pattern Book

Table Lanterns III

Designs & Photography
Hiroyuki Kobayashi & Jeffrey Castaline

Co-authored with
Vincent Dimas & Franci Claudon

ALL RIGHTS RESERVED The contents of this book may not be copied, reproduced or used in any manner in any commercial enterprise without the express written permission of the publisher. The contents of this book are for personal use only.

Copyright © Aanraku Stained Glass, 2002　　　I S B N 0-9716554-0-5

Distribution: Aanraku Stained Glass　　2323 S. El Camino Real, San Mateo, CA 94403-2213
www.BayAreaStainedglass.com　　Tel: (650) 372-0527, Fax (650) 372-0566
Email: aanraku@BayAreaStainedglass.com

Dedication

To my parents, Naoyuki and Mitsu Kobayashi.
With my love and respect.

Hiroyuki
Owner, Aanraku Stained Glass

About Us In the fall of 1997, Jeffrey Castaline and Hiroyuki Kobayashi opened the San Mateo, California studio **Aanraku Stained Glass**. It has grown past expectations.

The studio has about 200+ students floating around at any given time, and all of them, from their beginner's project on, are creating professional quality stained glass. There is nothing hard about doing stained glass. With the proper instruction anyone can do it and their student's work bears that out.

Jeffrey, originally from Boston, Massachusetts, has worked in art glass for nearly four decades. As a teen, he learned his neighbor was a stained glass artist. In time, the man let him cut a piece of glass and the die was cast.

Hiroyuki, from Tokyo, Japan, doesn't work in glass, but designs stained glass patterns. His eye for color leads students to seek his help in selecting glass.

The studio's classes are intensive, with a minimum of 200 glass pieces for beginners' work sometimes going up to 800 pieces. Students' beginning projects are professional quality.

Aanraku also publishes pattern books containing student's designs. About 90 percent of the studio's beginners are published artists.

CUSTOM PATTERN PRINTING SERVICE

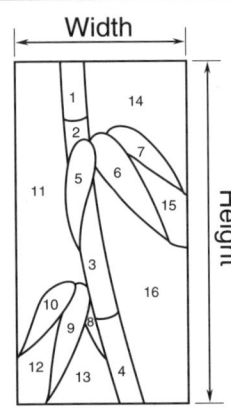

All the patterns in this book may be ordered, printed proportionally to a specific height or width, pre-numbered, with a color graphics work sheet and glass suggestions at a cost of $5.00 for the first linear ft., and $3.00 for each additional linear ft., per copy.

Custom sized patterns, both height & width, are available for the above fees plus a one time $10.00 resizing fee.

*Prices subject to change at any time without prior notice.

For additional information on patterns, design and printing, visit our web site at: **www.BayAreaStainedGlass.com** or email us at: **Aanraku@BayAreaStainedGlass.com**

Table Lamp Assembly (Fig 1.)

Components needed for the assembly of the electrical portion of the Table Lanterns are shown at the bottom of page 4.

1. First make the three panels needed for the front and back sides of the lantern. We recommend the sides be 6" wide and 12" tall, but you can make your lamp any size you like. All three panels have to be bordered around the outside with foil. We recommend 7/32" for best results. (Fig. 2.)

2. Tin the edges of all three panels with solder. Once assembled the inside edges where panels are joined cannot easily be reached with the tip of the soldering iron and pre-tinning the edges insures that the patina will take to all the edges evenly.

3. Stand two panels upright (Fig. 3.) and with a 3" x " strip of poster board creased in the middle and two paper clamps, hold them together. Position the third panel, and using the same technique secure the other two corners. Make minor adjustments to the clamps and panels until the inner edges of the panels are in alignment and there is a "V" opening at each corner. Gently align the bottom edges of the panel so all sides are uniform. Be sure the top edges of the panels are at the same height.

4. Flux the vertical seams where the panels come together. With a drop of solder on the tip of your soldering iron join all three panels on top of the corners. (Fig. 5.) After joining the tops, gently adjust the bottom of each vertical seam and tack the bottom corners one at time in turn until all three are done. With just a drop of solder tack one or two places along the side for stability. Repeat this tacking on all three vertical seams.

5. Remove the paper clamps and poster board pieces. Lay the lantern flat on one side. When laying flat on one side, one of the seams will be on top. (See fig. 6.) Holding the soldering iron thin edge down, turn down the heat of the iron so that solder melts but doesn't run. Take a gather on the end of the iron and begin building a bead along the seam. If there are spaces between the edges of the panels, trim and lay a strip of foil along the length of the gap and solder it in place to keep the solder forming the bead from dripping through. Use a chopping motion, pausing for 2~3 seconds between solder applications, to add and smooth the solder on the seams. DO NOT run along the length of the seam. Going along the seam will overheat the solder and cause the line to stay flat and run out between the glass panel edges.

6. After soldering all three seams, run a rounded bead on the foil on the top and bottom edges of the glass to reinforce them.

7. Prepare the legs of the lamp by cutting three 4" lengths of 1/8" diameter steel rod. Steel wool the full length and end of each steel leg until it is clean, shiny and free of oxidation. Lay down all three legs together, side by side and with a marker draw a thin line across all three rods in the middle to mark the soldering position. (Fig. 8.)

8. Lay The lamp on towels, books or other materials so that one seam is down on the bottom and the end of the lamp is angled up at a low angle so you can see down the inside of the seam. (See Fig. 7.) With one hand hold the leg rod flat along the inside of the seam with the marker mark in the middle of the foil line on the bottom edge of the panel intersection, then tack the top of the rod in place with a drop or two or solder. (Fig. 4-A) NOTE: DO NOT form a large glob on top of the leg to hold it in place. Only a small uniform tack drop is necessary. When installing the spider to hold the electrical, the arms of the spider will need to sit on top of the tack on the top of the leg. (Fig. 4-A).

9. Stand the lantern on end upside down and build a small mound of solder connected to the outer seam to give the leg strength and support. (Fig. 4-B upside down.) The top tack holding the leg is not strong. This bottom mound of solder tack is the main leg support. Be sure the solder completely surrounds the leg (360°)

10. After attaching and soldering all three legs in place, stand the lantern right side up and lay the 3-pronged spider on top. Mark the ends of the spider and cut them so when lowered into the top of the lantern the spider sits securely on top of the legs. Tack solder the spider in place. (Fig 4-A.)

11. Wash, patina and polish the lantern.

12. After finishing the lantern, prepare a triangular wood base, (8" on a side.). Finish if desired. Next, place the lantern on top of the finished base and very gently press down from the top to make a small depression under each leg. Remove lantern from the base and drill three 1/8" deep holes.

12. After assembling and installing the electrical components (Fig. 2.) place a single drop of glue in each hole in the base, set your lantern on the base and you are done.

Copyright ©2002 Aanraku Stained Glass

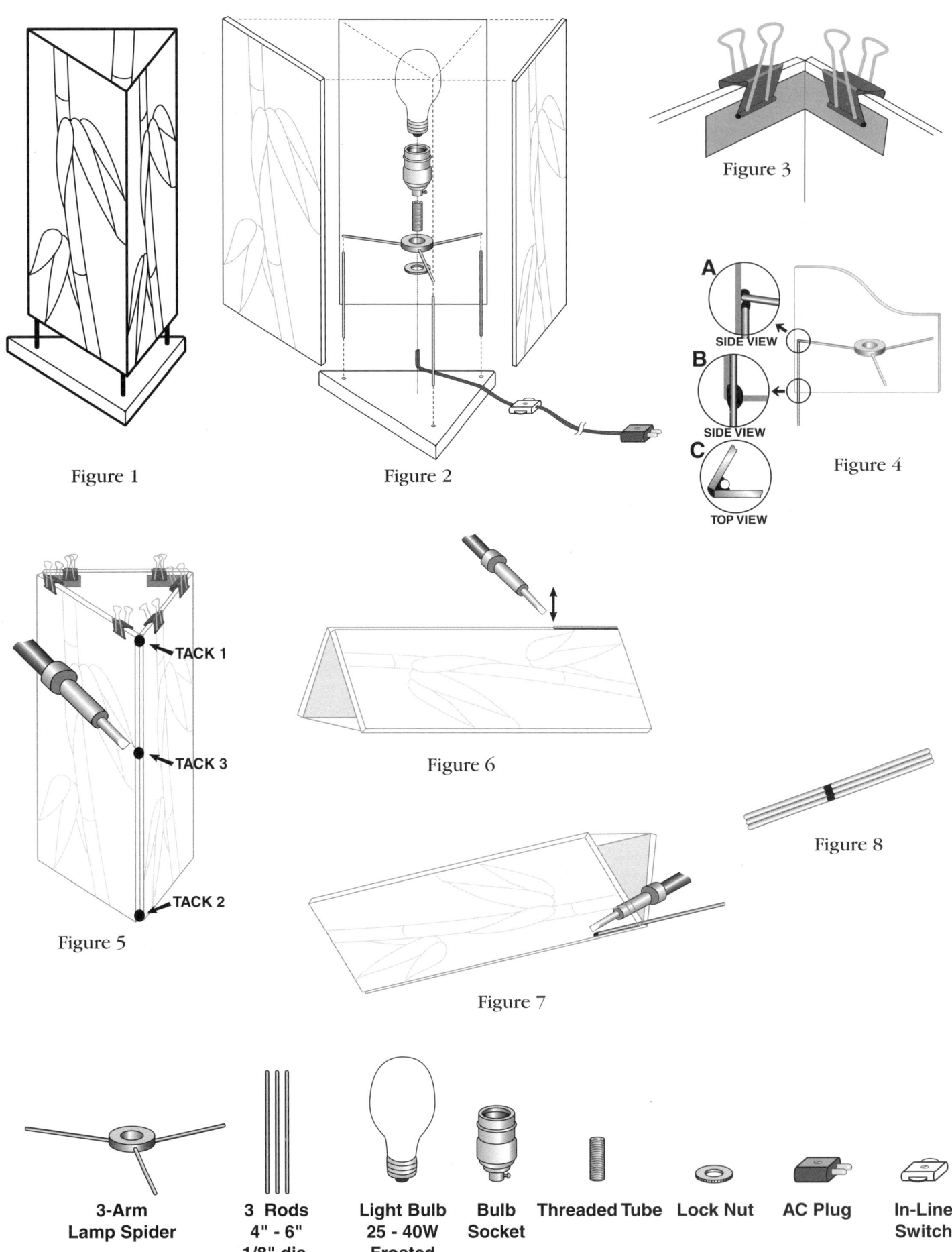

Figure 1

Figure 2

Figure 3

Figure 4

Figure 5

Figure 6

Figure 7

Figure 8

3-Arm Lamp Spider | 3 Rods 4" - 6" 1/8" dia. | Light Bulb 25 - 40W Frosted | Bulb Socket | Threaded Tube | Lock Nut | AC Plug | In-Line Switch

Ai - Love   33 pieces

Enlarge: 126%

First rendering by Franci Claudon

Copyright ©2002 Aanraku Stained Glass

AngelFish

65 pieces

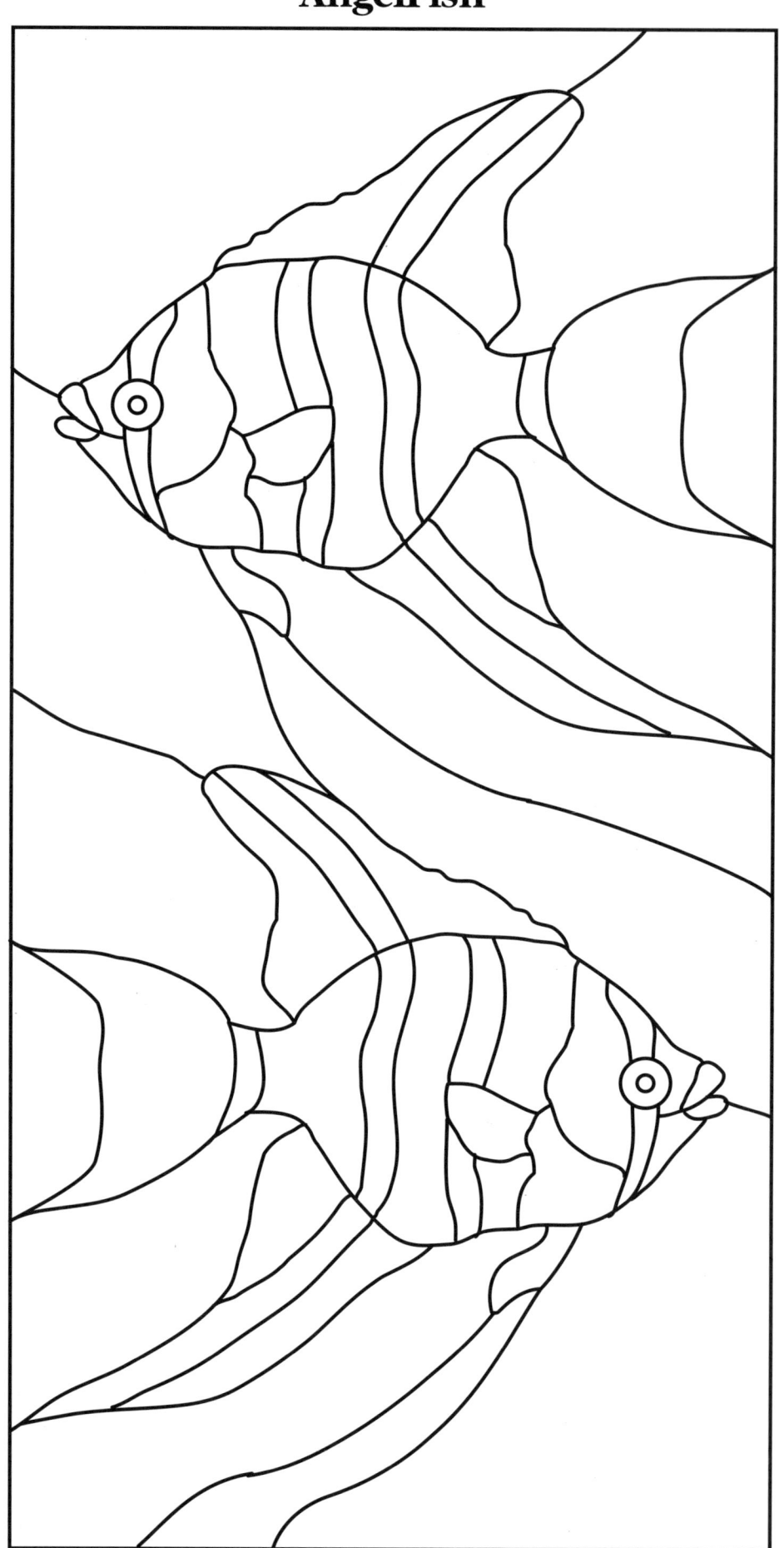

Enlarge: 126%

First rendering by Greg Gentile

Copyright ©2002 Aanraku Stained Glass

Chameleon (2 panels) 59 pieces total

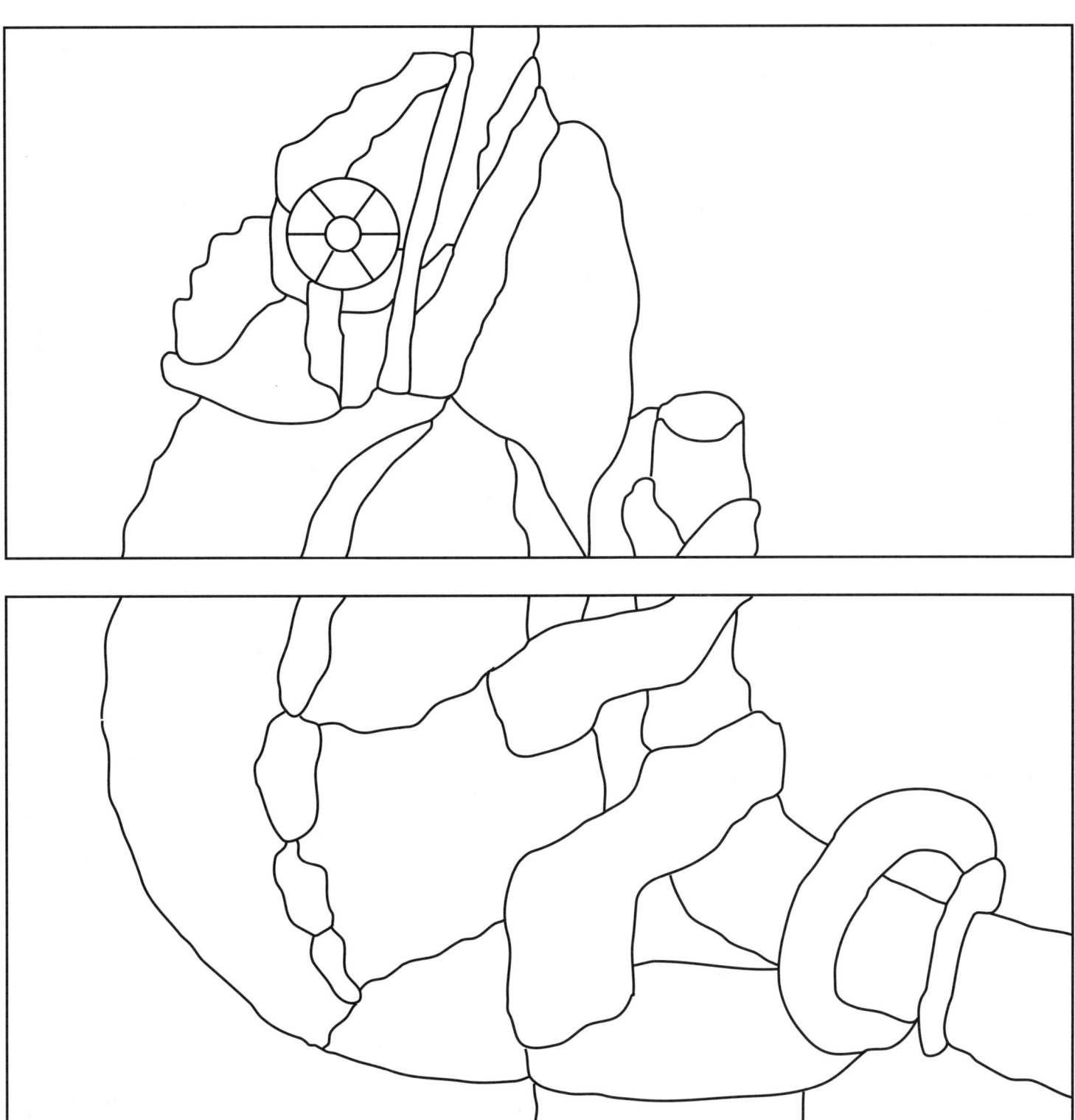

Enlarge: 160% *First rendering by Barbara Berne*

Cardinal 45 pieces

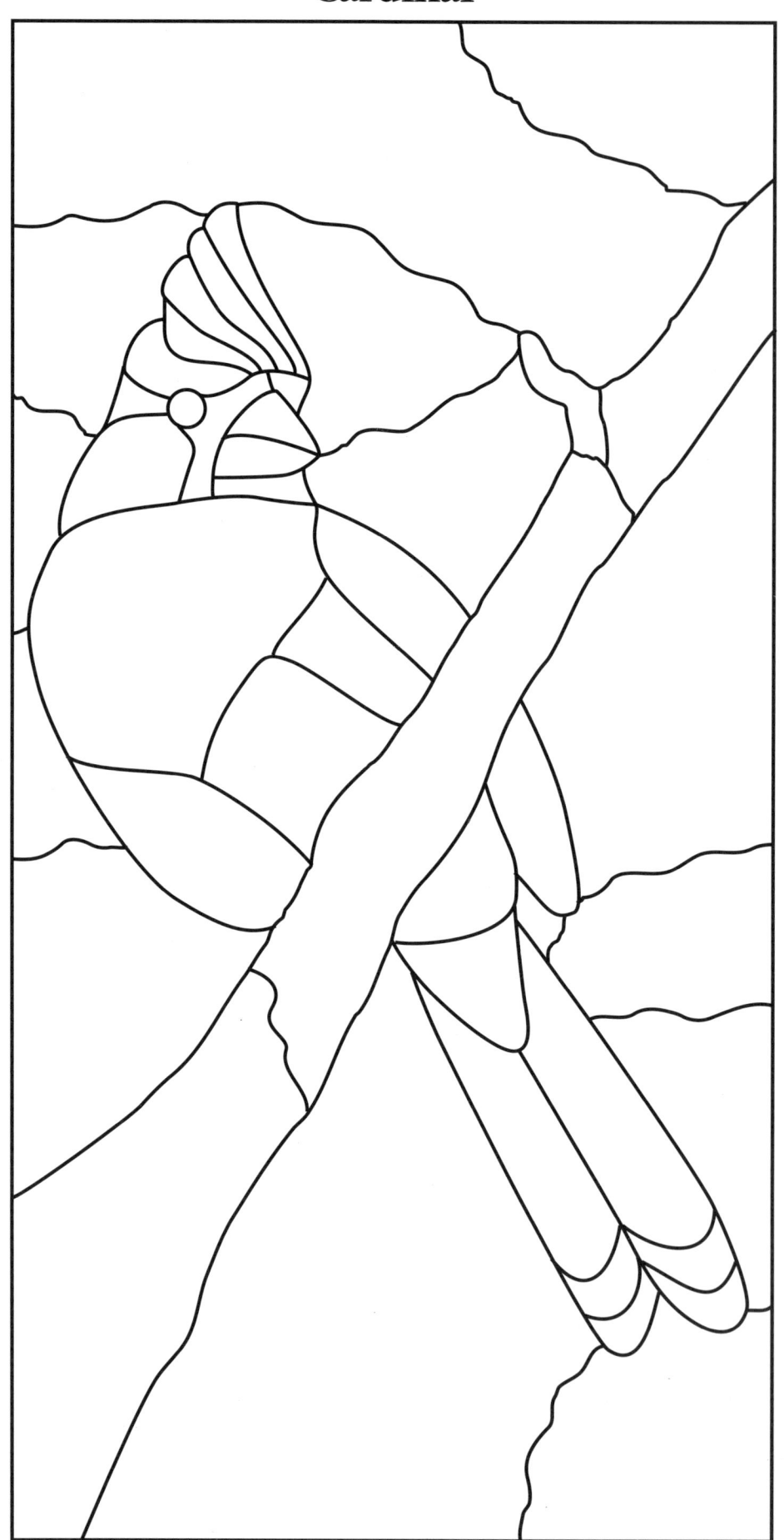

Enlarge: 126%

First rendering by Franci Claudon

Chicks 32 pieces

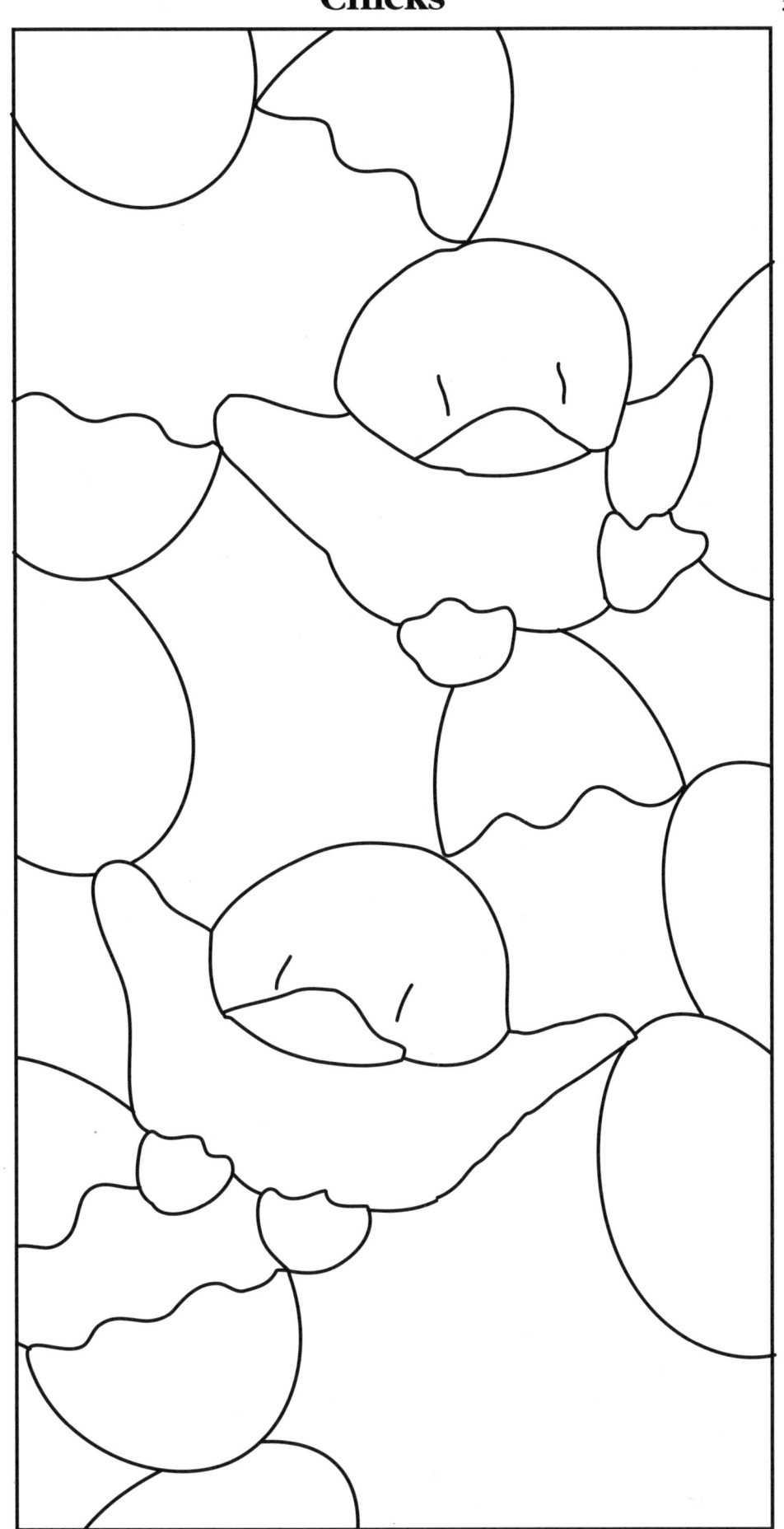

Enlarge: 126%

First rendering by Franci Claudon

Cypress (3 panels) — 74 pieces total

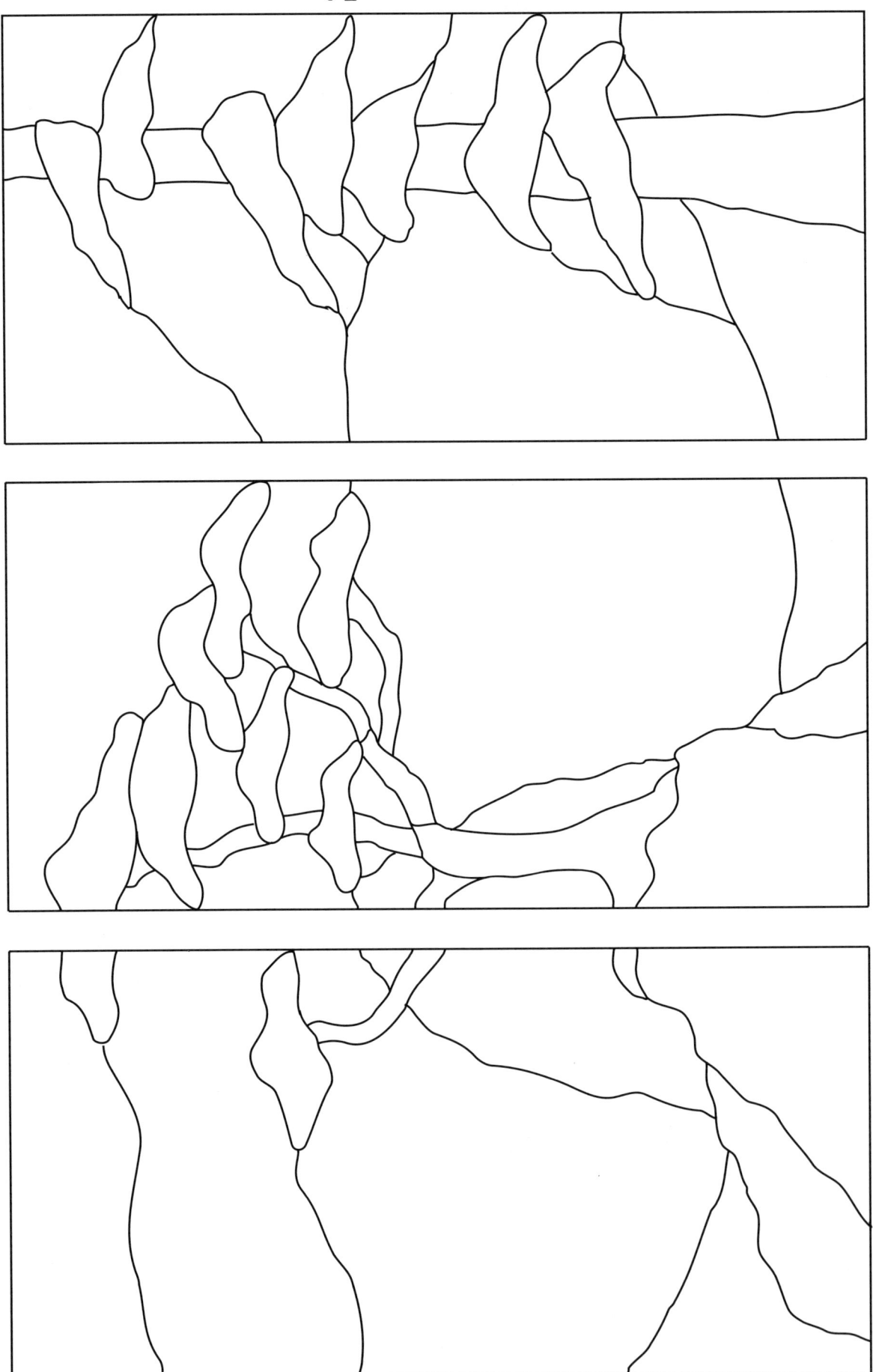

Enlarge: 201%

Design and first rendering by Steph Thompson

Ducks

26 pieces

Enlarge: 126%

First rendering by Vincent Dimas

Copyright ©2002 Aanraku Stained Glass

Fuji
18 pieces

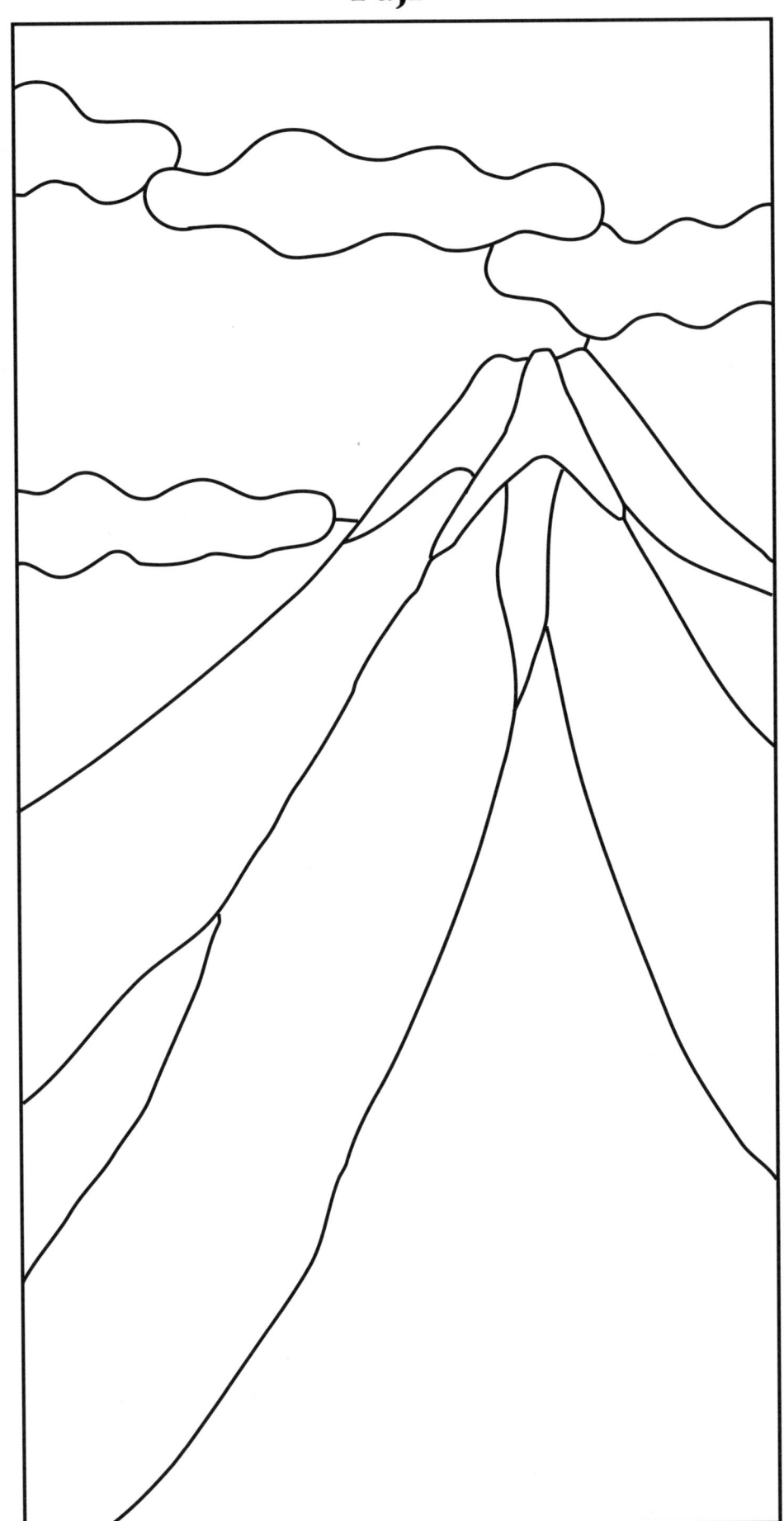

Enlarge: 126%

First rendering by Tara Cazaubon

Green Fairy **58 pieces**

Enlarge: 126% *First rendering by Tracy Molitor*

Haloween

25 pieces

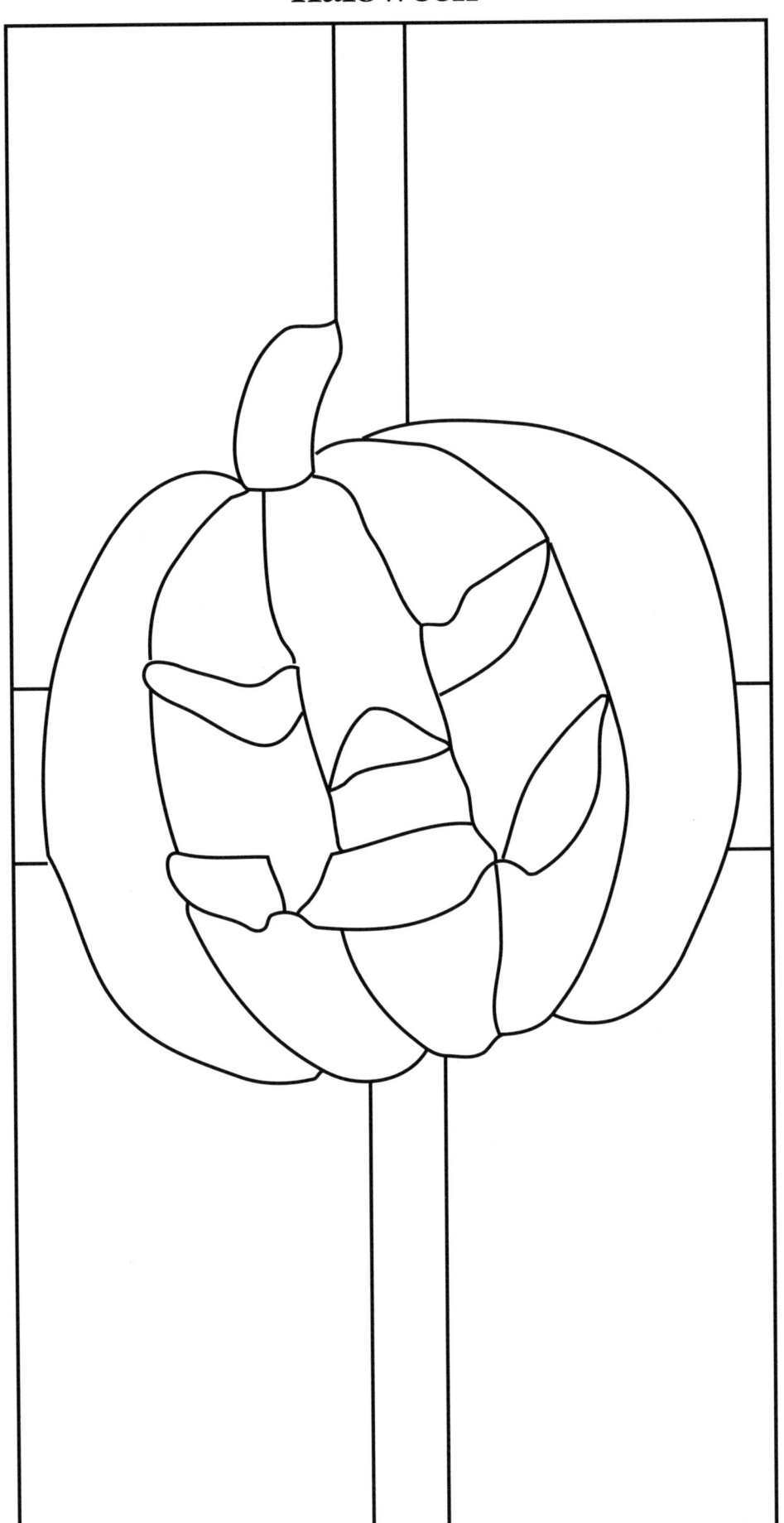

Enlarge: 126%

First rendering by Vincent Dimas

Copyright ©2002 Aanraku Stained Glass

Iris

42 pieces

Enlarge: 126%

First rendering by Ivy Tong

Copyright ©2002 Aanraku Stained Glass

- 15 -

Kingfisher   42 pieces

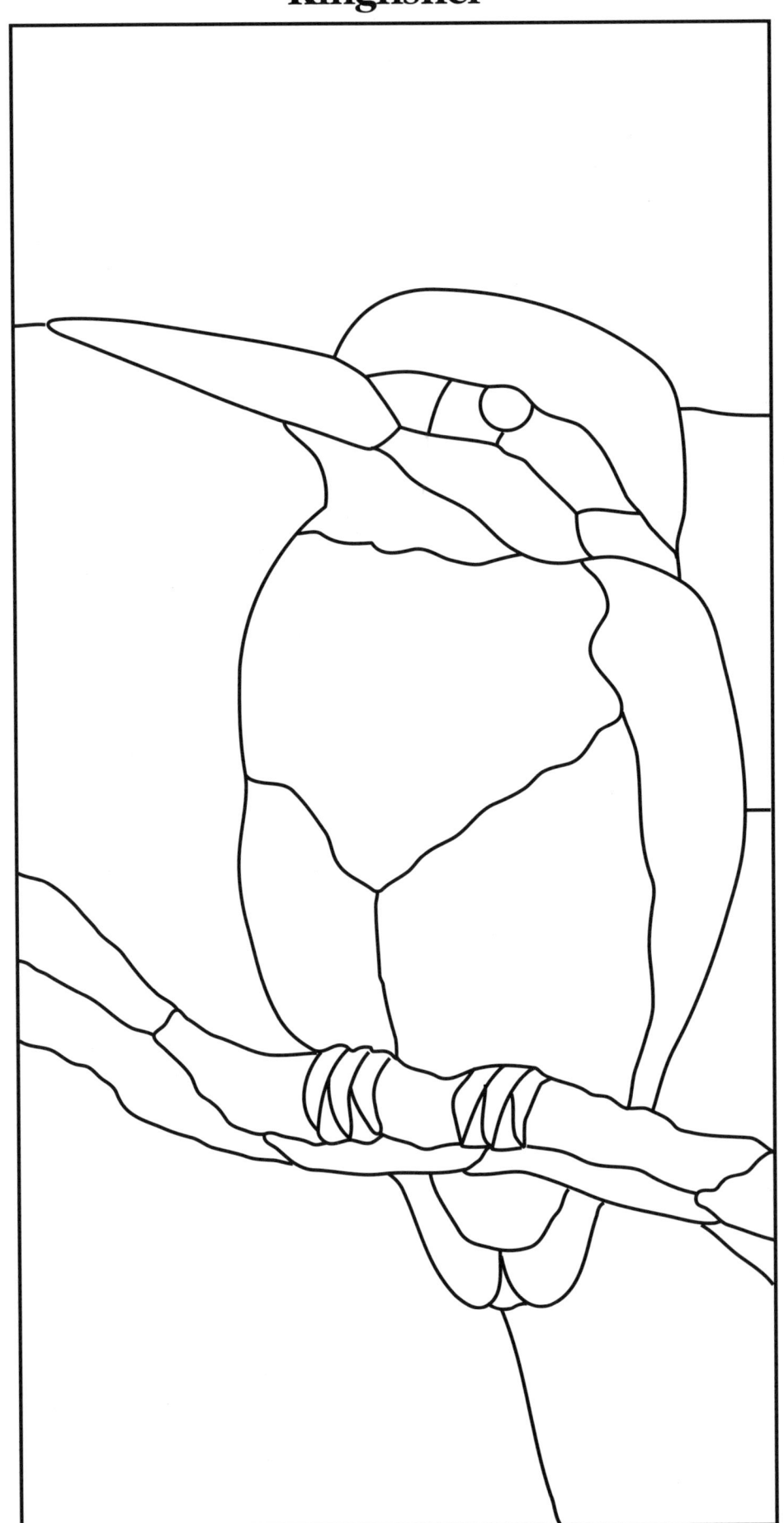

Enlarge: 126%

- 16 -   Copyright ©2002 Aanraku Stained Glass

Lighthouse

39 pieces

Enlarge: 126%

First rendering by Vincent Dimas

Copyright ©2002 Aanraku Stained Glass

Meiwakuccino

55 pieces

Enlarge: 126%

- 18 -

Copyright ©2002 Aanraku Stained Glass

Mice

35 pieces

Enlarge: 126%

First rendering by Vincent Dimas

Copyright ©2002 Aanraku Stained Glass

Morning Glory   46 pieces

Enlarge: 126%

First rendering by Masaru Imada

Oak

24 pieces

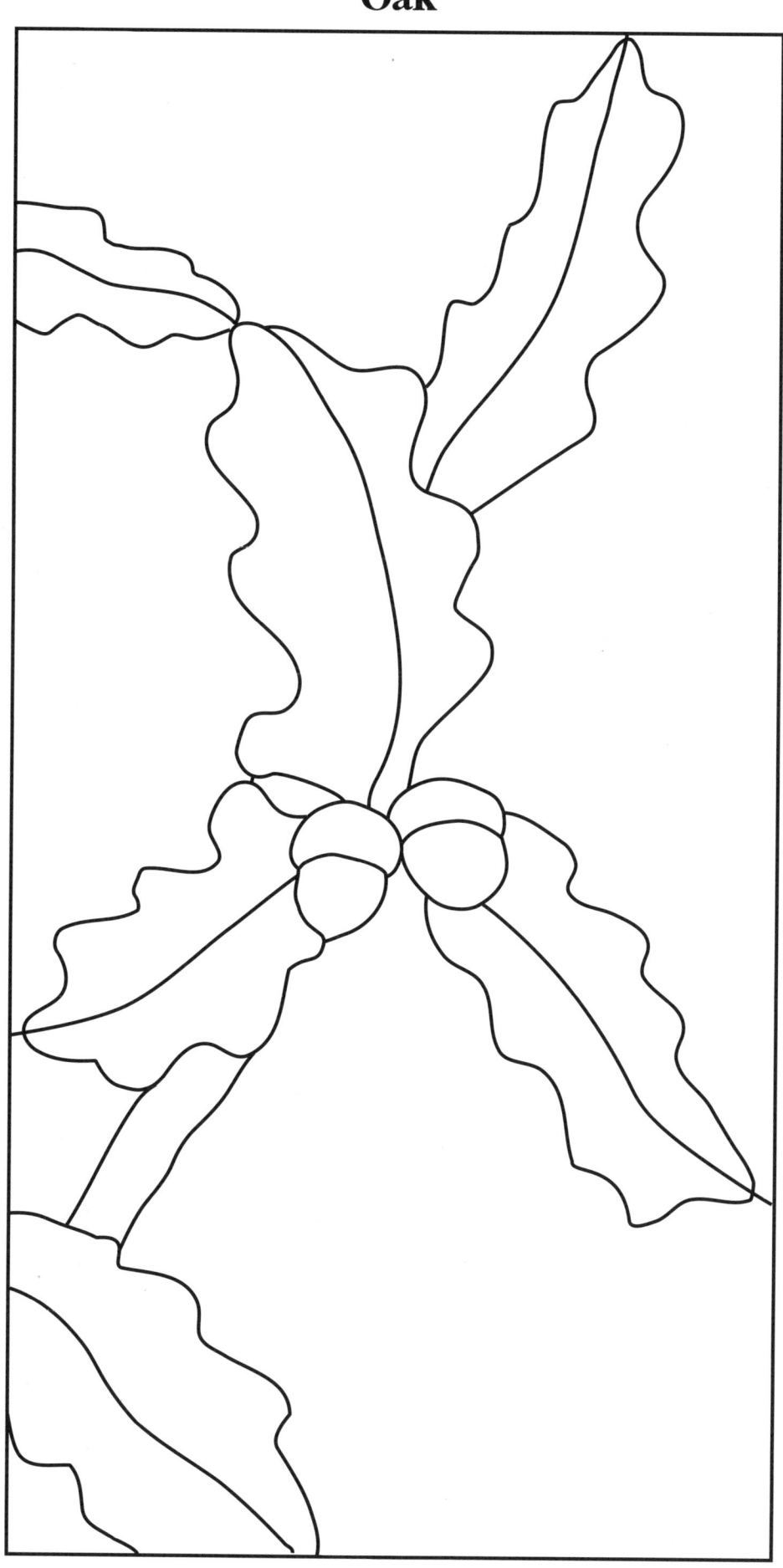

Enlarge: 126%

Orchid **38 pieces**

Enlarge: 126%

First rendering by Franci Claudon

Paper Plane

23 pieces

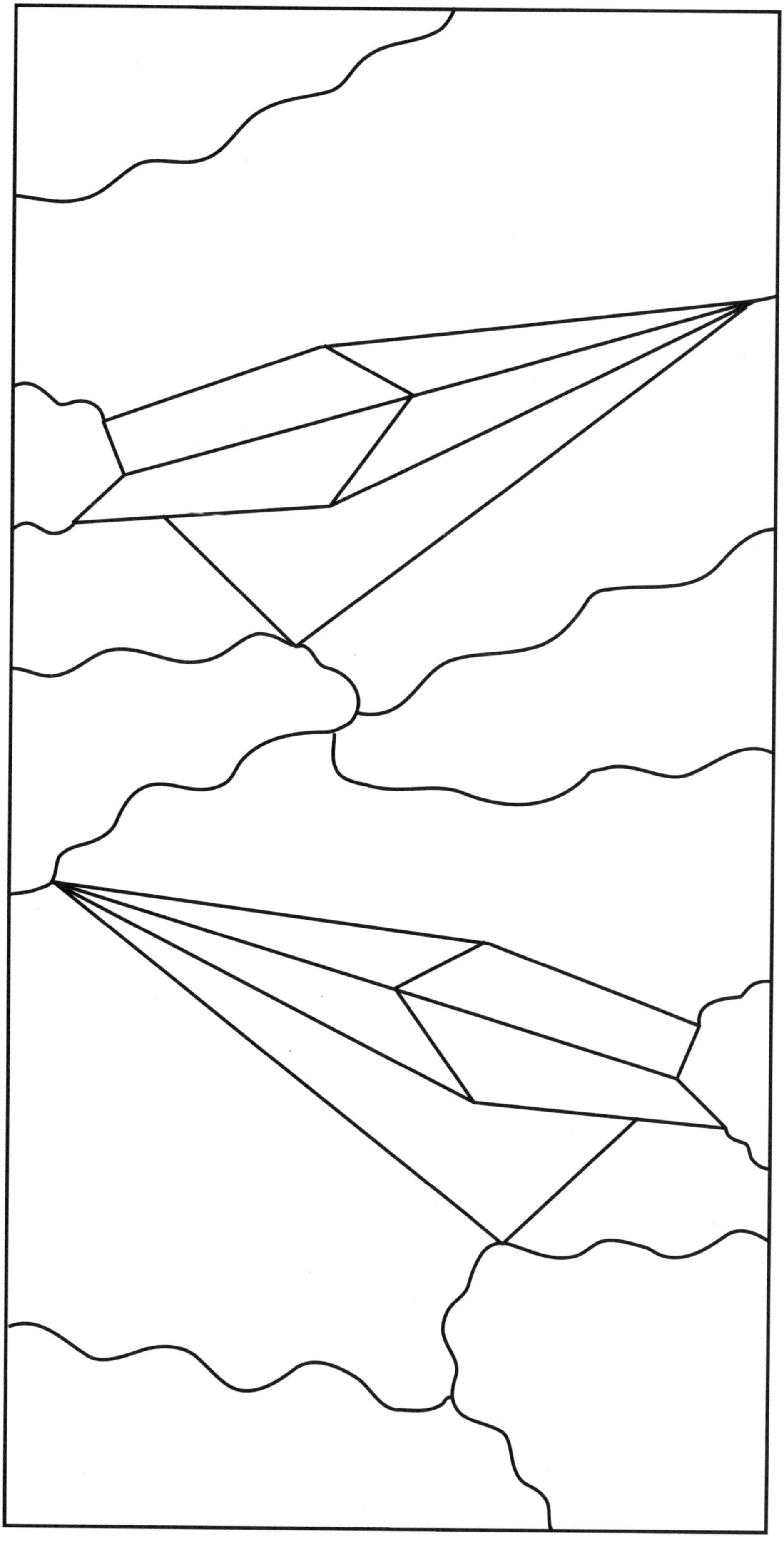

Enlarge: 126%

Platypus 42 pieces

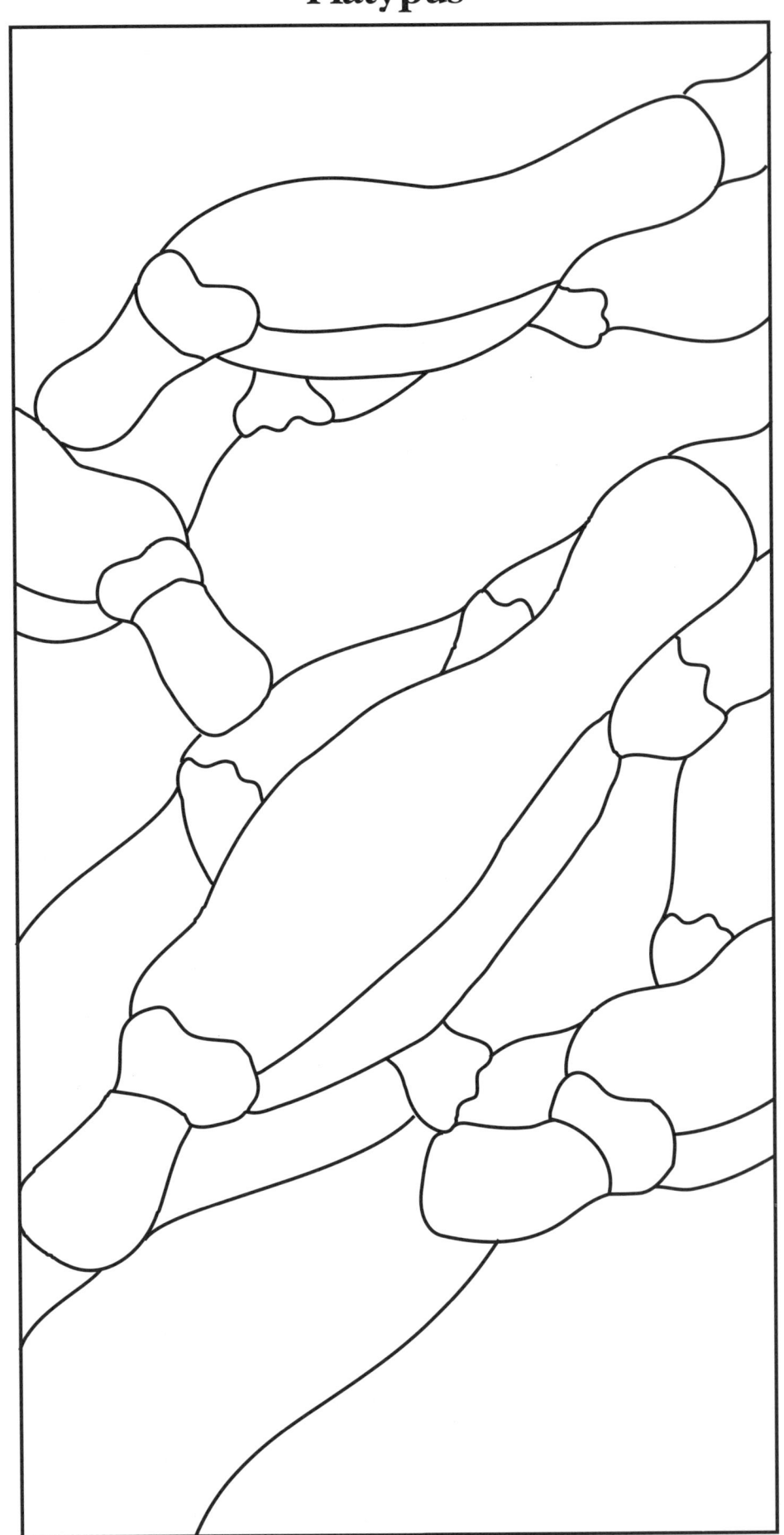

Enlarge: 195%

First rendering by Glenn Ware

Sailing Boats (3 panels)   87 pieces total

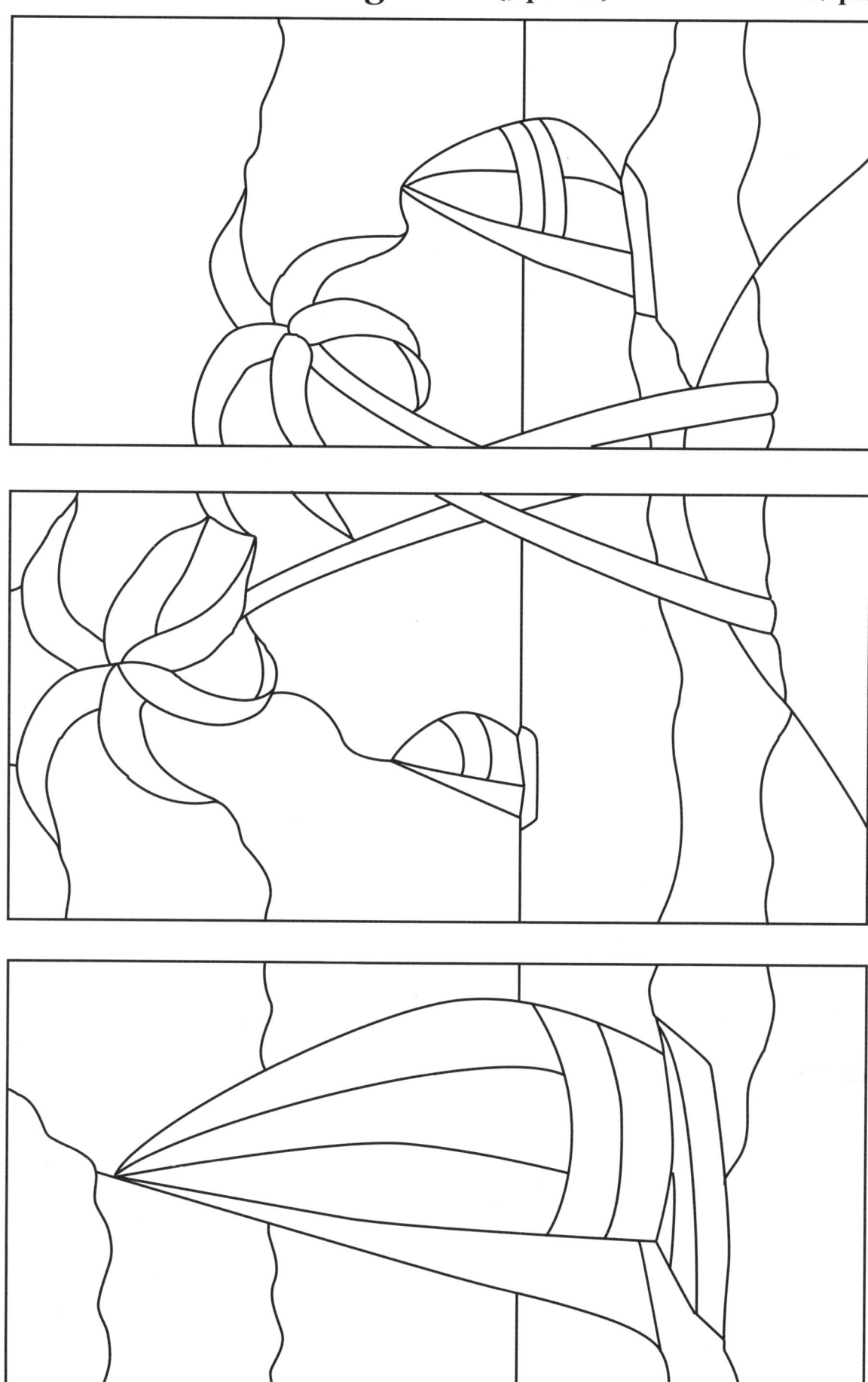

Enlarge: 201%   *Design and first rendering by Steph Thompson*

Santa Claus **62 pieces**

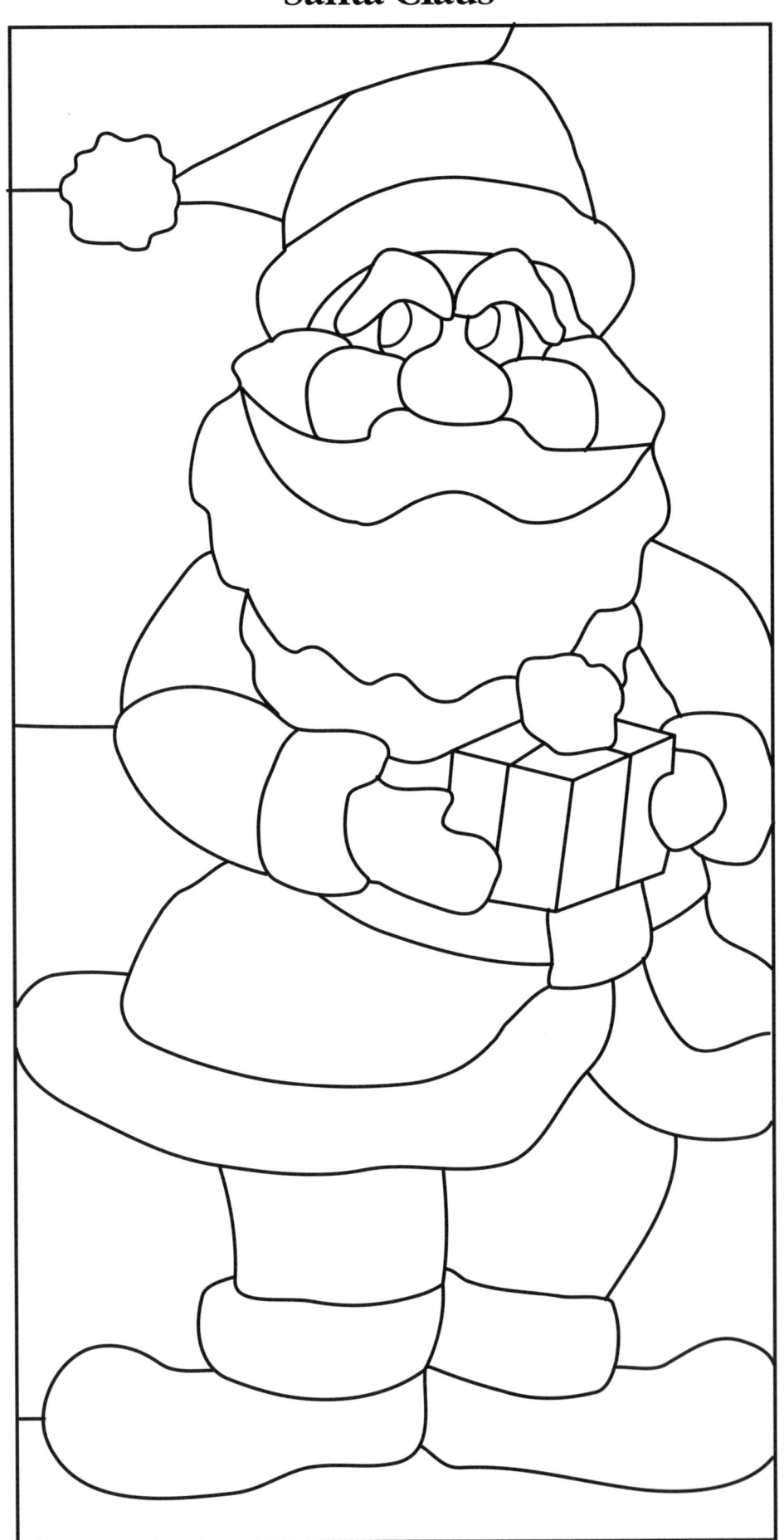

Enlarge: 126%

- 26 -

Copyright ©2002 Aanraku Stained Glass

First rendering by Vincent Dimas

Shiawase - Happy 47 pieces

Enlarge: 126% *First rendering by Vincent Dimas*

Sun & Moon (2 panels)   70 pieces total

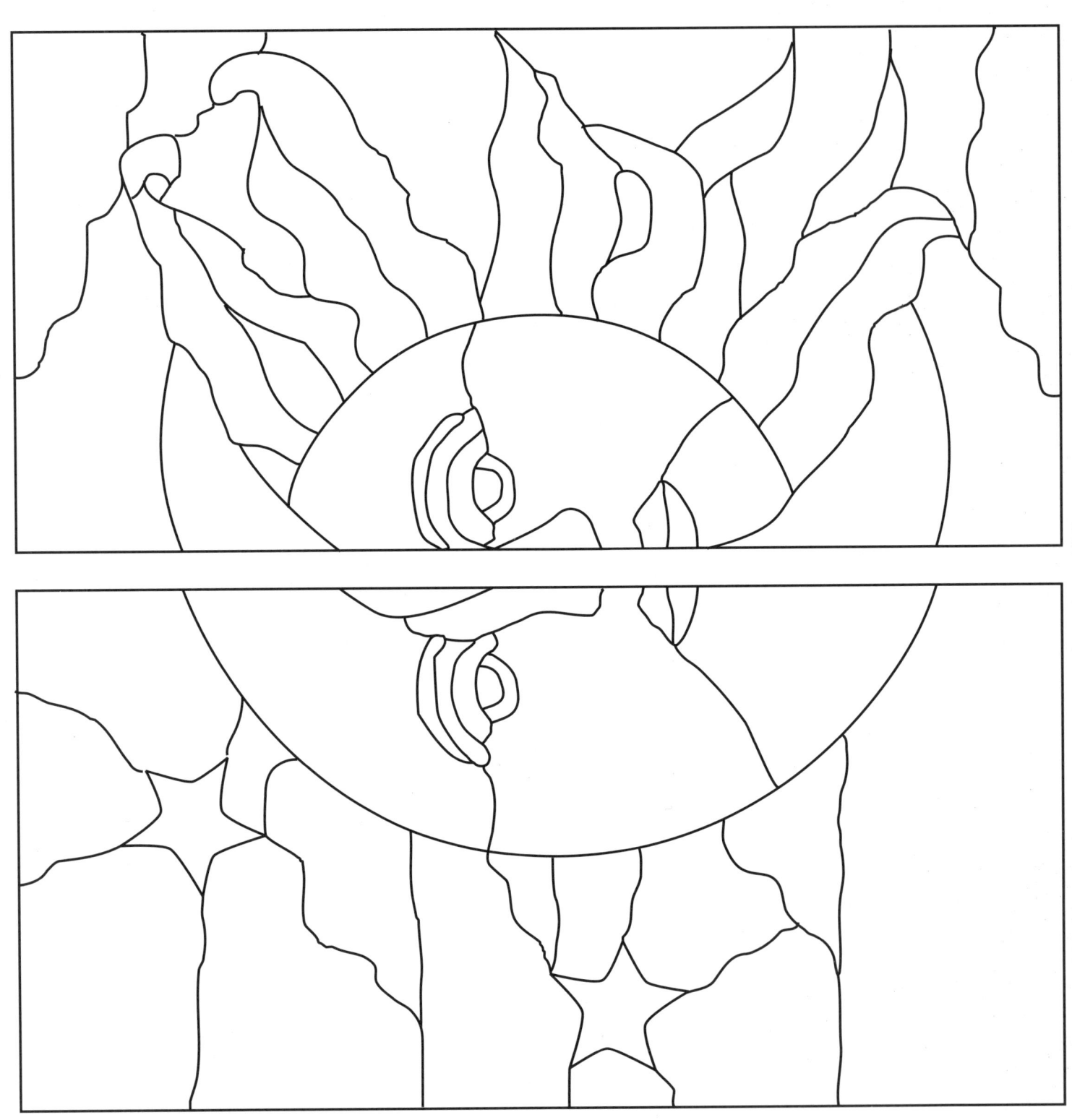

Enlarge: 160%

First rendering by Franci Claudon

Orchid - P.22

Lighthouse - P.17

Sun & Moon - P.28

Green Fairy - P.13

Chameleon - P.7

Oak - P.21